The Modern Product Owner

Skills to Navigate the Agile Work and Achieve Business and Product Strategy

TJ Rerob

The Modern Product Owner

Skills to Navigate the Agile Work and Achieve Business and Product Strategy

TJ Rerob

Table of Contents

Introduction

In the vast realm of technological progress, there are few breakthroughs as profound as quantum computing. While classical computers have powered the digital age, solving increasingly complex problems, they have reached the limits of their capabilities. The promise of quantum computing lies in its potential to leap beyond these limitations, offering a new way of processing information. Unlike traditional computers, which rely on bits as the smallest unit of data, quantum computers harness the power of quantum bits, or qubits. These qubits are not bound by the binary constraints of 0s and 1s; instead, they can exist in multiple states simultaneously, thanks to the strange, yet powerful, principles of quantum mechanics.

The ability of quantum computers to perform calculations in parallel, using superposition and entanglement, means they can solve problems that are currently unsolvable by classical machines. Tasks such as simulating molecular structures for drug discovery, optimizing complex systems, or breaking encryption methods are just a few of the many applications where quantum computing promises to make a seismic impact. The scale of what quantum computers can achieve has the potential to redefine industries and revolutionize the way we approach challenges in science, technology, and beyond.

However, the road to practical quantum computing has been long and filled with both immense challenges and extraordinary progress. The journey began with fundamental research into quantum mechanics and computing theories, but it wasn't until the late 20th century that scientists began to consider the practical implications of harnessing quantum states for computation. Early quantum computers were rudimentary and could only demonstrate basic principles. Over time, technological advancements pushed the boundaries, and by the early 2000s, the world saw the first tentative steps toward building real quantum processors. Yet, these early models were far from being useful in real-world applications.

Enter Google's Willow chip—an innovation that stands as a true game-changer in the quantum computing space. After years of incremental advancements, Google's Quantum AI division has achieved something that once seemed nearly impossible: the development of a quantum chip that can outperform classical computers in certain specialized tasks. Willow represents a culmination of years of research, refinement, and technological breakthroughs. But its importance goes beyond being just another quantum chip; Willow is the manifestation of a quantum computing system that can scale and solve problems previously thought to be intractable by classical machines.

The breakthrough brought by Willow lies not only in its ability to execute quantum algorithms faster than any previous chip but in its unique features that push the boundaries of what we thought was possible in quantum computing. With advancements such as dramatically increased quantum coherence times and sophisticated error correction methods, Willow has set the stage for a new era of quantum systems that could eventually lead to practical, large-scale quantum computers capable of solving some of the world's most complex and pressing problems. As Google's team continues to build upon Willow, it's clear that we are entering a new phase in the evolution of quantum computing, one that will shape the future in ways that are just beginning to be understood.

This chapter sets the stage for understanding why Willow is more than just a milestone in the development of quantum technology. It's a pivotal moment in a journey that has the potential to change the course of technology itself. From a deeper understanding of how quantum computing works to an exploration of how Willow opens new doors for research, industry, and innovation, this book will guide you through the groundbreaking advances of Google's Willow chip and explore its significance in the world of tomorrow. As you read, you will see how this quantum leap is not just about pushing the boundaries of computation but about transforming how we think about problem-solving and innovation in the 21st century.

Chapter 1: The Journey to Willow

Julian Kelly's journey into the world of quantum computing is a testament to the vision and ambition that Google has brought to this revolutionary field. As the director of hardware at Google Quantum AI, Kelly has been a key player in shaping the company's mission to build quantum computers that could solve problems beyond the reach of today's most powerful classical supercomputers. His interest in quantum computing began in 2008 when he first experimented with qubits—small units of quantum information. By 2015, Kelly joined Google, drawn by the company's audacious vision to develop a machine capable of solving computational problems that no current technology could even begin to address. This vision was not just about making quantum computers a reality; it was about shaping the future of computation itself.

Google's quantum computing initiative, which began as a small research project, quickly gained momentum under Kelly's leadership. At the heart of Google's quantum research was the understanding that quantum computing had the potential to revolutionize industries by enabling faster, more efficient solutions to problems in fields ranging from medicine and chemistry to logistics and artificial intelligence. But for all its promise, quantum computing was still in its infancy, and the road to practical application was fraught with technical hurdles. Google's approach, however, was built on steady, incremental progress. By advancing step by step, Google aimed not only to make quantum computing work but also to prove that it could outperform classical computers on meaningful tasks.

The first significant milestone in Google's quantum journey came in 2017 with the launch of *Foxtail*, the company's first quantum processor. While Foxtail was a breakthrough, it was still a relatively small and early example of what quantum computing could do. The real turning point came in 2018 with the release of *Bristol Cone*, a chip designed to solve more complex problems. By then, Google had already begun to push the limits of what was considered possible for quantum systems. Bristol Cone represented a leap forward in both the number of qubits and the reliability of those qubits, though challenges around coherence times remained.

In 2019, Google reached what is perhaps its most significant milestone at the time with *Sycamore*, a quantum processor designed to demonstrate the power of quantum supremacy—the idea that a quantum computer could solve a problem faster than the best classical supercomputers. This achievement was a defining moment in quantum computing history. Google's Sycamore processor solved a complex random circuit sampling problem in just 200 seconds, a task that, according to calculations, would have taken a classical supercomputer 10,000 years to complete. This success sent shockwaves through the scientific community, as it marked the first time a quantum computer had definitively outperformed a classical machine in a meaningful way.

However, while Sycamore's success in surpassing classical supercomputers was groundbreaking, it also highlighted the limitations that quantum computers still faced. Quantum coherence—the ability of qubits to maintain their quantum state long enough to perform calculations—remained a significant challenge. Sycamore's qubits could only maintain their coherence for a short time, meaning that while it could perform certain tasks exponentially faster than classical computers, the technology was still not ready for large-scale, general-purpose computation. The need for longer coherence times and more reliable error correction methods became increasingly clear as the field advanced.

It was this understanding that led directly to Willow. Building on the success of Sycamore, Willow sought to address one of the major hurdles in quantum computing: coherence time. While Sycamore had laid the foundation by demonstrating quantum supremacy in a narrow context, Willow's goal was to create a more stable, scalable quantum chip that could support larger, more complex computations and, crucially, solve the issues related to coherence. Willow's design incorporated new materials, architectures, and fabrication techniques that allowed for a significant increase in coherence times—five times longer than Sycamore's. This breakthrough was critical not just for pushing the boundaries of quantum computing but for making large-scale quantum systems a practical reality.

Looking back at the evolution of Google's quantum chips, each iteration has provided important lessons that paved the way for Willow's success. From Foxtail's modest beginnings to the ambitious goals of Bristol Cone and the historic achievements of Sycamore, each chip has contributed to a deeper understanding of the technical challenges and solutions required for building quantum computers that can operate at scale. Along the way, Google has learned how to better manage qubit connectivity, reduce error rates, and refine the overall architecture of its quantum processors. Each of these lessons has been vital in the development of Willow, which represents the latest and most advanced quantum chip from Google.

Willow's significance lies in how it builds on these past successes while addressing the key challenges that remained unsolved. By taking the lessons learned from Sycamore and combining them with new innovations in quantum coherence and error correction, Willow sets the stage for the next phase of quantum computing. It's a step closer to realizing the dream of a large-scale, fault-tolerant quantum computer capable of tackling real-world problems—ushering in a future where quantum technologies are no longer confined to the lab, but are transforming industries and solving the world's most pressing challenges.

Chapter 2: Willow – The New Frontier

Willow represents a quantum leap in the development of quantum computing. As Google's most powerful quantum chip to date, it embodies the next step in the company's ambitious goal of building large-scale, practical quantum computers. At its core, Willow is designed to solve the limitations that have hindered earlier quantum systems, such as Sycamore, by addressing the critical issue of quantum coherence. It combines innovative architectural improvements with cutting-edge quantum technology to move quantum computing closer to real-world applications. The chip's superconducting design allows it to operate at extremely low temperatures, enabling the manipulation of qubits with unprecedented accuracy and efficiency. This technological leap is not just about increasing computational power—it's about making quantum systems stable enough to scale and solve more complex problems.

The development of Willow is rooted in Google's broader vision to create quantum computers that can handle tasks far beyond the reach of classical supercomputers. Google's previous quantum chips, such as Sycamore, demonstrated remarkable potential but faced fundamental limitations in maintaining quantum coherence. These limitations were a significant obstacle in achieving the level of performance necessary for large-scale computations. Willow overcomes this barrier, making a substantial leap forward in coherence times—an essential factor for practical quantum computation.

Quantum coherence is a phenomenon at the heart of quantum computing. It refers to the ability of quantum bits, or qubits, to maintain their quantum state long enough to perform computations. In classical computing, bits are always in one state—either 0 or 1. But qubits, thanks to the principles of quantum mechanics, can exist in multiple states simultaneously due to superposition. For qubits to perform useful calculations, however, they need to remain in a coherent state long enough to manipulate and process information. The longer the coherence time, the more complex calculations a quantum computer can perform. Short coherence times limit the usefulness of quantum computers by restricting the number of operations that can be carried out before the qubits lose their quantum properties.

With Willow, Google has taken a huge step toward resolving this challenge. By enhancing coherence times by a factor of five, Willow's qubits can now maintain their state for 100 microseconds, compared to Sycamore's 20 microseconds. This seemingly small increase has massive implications for the capabilities of quantum systems. Longer coherence times allow for more operations, enabling the chip to process more complex calculations without losing accuracy. For quantum computers to scale, this improvement in coherence time is a crucial milestone. It opens up the possibility for more sophisticated algorithms, better error correction, and, ultimately, quantum machines that can solve problems too complex for classical computers to handle.

At the heart of Willow's design are superconducting qubits. Superconducting qubits are created using materials that, when cooled to extremely low temperatures, exhibit zero electrical resistance, allowing them to maintain quantum states with greater stability. These qubits are the building blocks of Willow, and their superconducting nature is what allows the chip to operate with such high efficiency. Superconducting qubits are also highly tunable, meaning they can be manipulated with precision to achieve the desired computational results. The ability to control the behavior of these qubits in such a detailed manner is what sets Willow apart from earlier quantum chips.

Willow builds upon the technology that was introduced with Sycamore but takes it to the next level. While Sycamore demonstrated that quantum computers could outperform classical machines in certain tasks, it was limited by relatively short coherence times and a lack of scalability. Willow overcomes these limitations by leveraging new materials and fabrication techniques to create a chip that is not only more stable but also more scalable. By increasing coherence times, Willow enables error correction techniques to become more effective, allowing for larger, more complex quantum systems to be built and operated reliably.

In essence, Willow is a product of years of technological refinement. The lessons learned from earlier quantum chips, including the Sycamore chip, have been instrumental in driving the design of Willow. Each advancement has brought Google closer to solving the fundamental challenges of quantum computing, and Willow represents a breakthrough that makes large-scale quantum computing not just a possibility, but an approaching reality. With this chip, Google has made significant strides in moving quantum computing from the realm of theoretical physics into the practical domain, setting the stage for a future where quantum computers can solve problems of immense complexity in fields like drug discovery, climate modeling, and artificial intelligence.

The breakthrough represented by Willow is more than just an incremental improvement—it's a transformational step that will shape the future of computing for years to come.

Chapter 3: The Role of Quantum Error Correction

One of the greatest challenges in the field of quantum computing is the issue of quantum errors. Unlike classical computers, which can correct errors in a reliable and predictable manner, quantum computers face a unique set of challenges. The quantum states that qubits represent are highly susceptible to disturbances from their environment, a phenomenon known as *decoherence*. Even the smallest interference—such as temperature fluctuations, electromagnetic noise, or stray photons—can cause qubits to lose their quantum state, resulting in errors. This is where quantum error correction becomes a critical element in building a practical and reliable quantum computer.

Quantum error correction is essential because, in a quantum system, errors are not just random glitches that can be fixed through simple methods. Due to the fragile nature of quantum states, when a qubit errors, it can corrupt the information of the entire computation, leading to widespread inaccuracies. The challenge is further compounded by the fact that quantum errors are fundamentally different from classical errors. In classical computing, an error in a bit can be detected, corrected, and the system can move forward. But in quantum computing, measurement itself disturbs the system, meaning that simply reading the state of a qubit can cause an error. This makes error correction much more complex and difficult to implement.

The importance of effective error correction cannot be overstated. Without it, quantum computers would be unreliable and unable to perform computations over extended periods of time or on a large scale. To make quantum computers useful for practical applications, we need to develop techniques that can correct these errors without undermining the very advantages that quantum systems offer. This has been one of the key barriers in the field, and until recently, it seemed that quantum error correction was something only possible in theory.

This is where Willow makes a groundbreaking contribution. Google's Willow chip has made a significant leap forward in quantum error correction by operating below the quantum error correction threshold. This is a monumental achievement because it means that Willow can perform quantum computations with error rates low enough that the errors can be managed and corrected effectively. The breakthrough is not just in the reduction of errors but in how these errors are dealt with at scale.

One of the key aspects of Willow's success is its ability to *suppress errors exponentially* with the addition of more qubits. In quantum computing, the concept of logical qubits is crucial. Logical qubits are essentially "virtual qubits" that are created by combining multiple physical qubits. The more physical qubits you add to a logical qubit, the more you can correct errors. Each additional qubit improves the accuracy and reliability of the system, and with Willow's design, errors are exponentially suppressed as more qubits are added. This principle is a critical step toward achieving fault-tolerant quantum computing—the idea that a quantum computer can continue to perform accurate computations even in the presence of errors.

The progress that Willow has made in this area cannot be underestimated. By enabling the creation of logical qubits that maintain their accuracy despite the underlying errors of the physical qubits, Willow has created a path toward quantum systems that can scale up without suffering from the loss of precision that plagued earlier designs. This advancement makes it more feasible to create large-scale, functional quantum computers that can handle real-world applications, ranging from optimization problems to simulations of complex molecular structures.

The concept of quantum error correction has been a theoretical pursuit for decades. In the 1990s, physicists began to develop ideas around how to protect quantum information from errors, drawing on principles from coding theory and quantum mechanics. Early theoretical work suggested that it was possible to protect quantum information by encoding it in multiple qubits. However, implementing these ideas in practice proved to be far more challenging. The problem was not just about encoding information but also about dealing with the inherent noise and errors that arise in a quantum system. Researchers had to overcome both theoretical and engineering challenges to make quantum error correction a viable solution.

For years, these theories remained largely theoretical, with few practical applications. But with Willow, Google has successfully applied these ideas to create a functioning quantum system that can operate with reliable accuracy. The chip's ability to suppress errors at scale and create logical qubits that maintain coherence is a direct application of the quantum error correction principles first outlined in the 90s.

Willow's success demonstrates that it is now possible to move from theory to practice, achieving error-free quantum computation in real-world systems.

This leap forward in error correction brings quantum computing closer to the reality of large-scale, practical quantum systems. With Willow, Google has moved beyond the realm of basic quantum experiments into the territory of truly usable quantum computers. The breakthrough in error correction means that quantum computers can now solve problems that classical computers cannot handle, with a reliability that was previously thought to be unattainable. This achievement represents not only a technical success but also a philosophical shift in how we think about the future of computing. What was once a distant dream is now within our reach, thanks to Willow's application of quantum error correction, bringing us one step closer to a future where quantum computers play a central role in solving some of the world's most complex problems.

Chapter 4: Performance Benchmarking – Willow vs. Supercomputers

Random circuit sampling is a benchmark used to demonstrate the capabilities of quantum computers, particularly their ability to perform tasks that are practically impossible for classical computers. In essence, random circuit sampling involves generating and sampling the outputs of quantum circuits that are chosen randomly. These circuits are complex enough that no classical algorithm can solve the problem efficiently, but quantum computers, with their unique ability to exploit superposition and entanglement, can handle them much more effectively.

The random circuit sampling benchmark serves as a litmus test for quantum computers, allowing researchers to compare their performance against classical systems. The importance of this benchmark is twofold. First, it helps to measure the quantum computer's ability to produce truly random outputs from quantum states, a task that exploits the principles of quantum mechanics in a way that classical algorithms cannot. Second, it provides a tangible measure of a quantum computer's superiority over classical systems in solving specific types of problems that would otherwise be intractable for classical machines.

Willow's performance in this benchmark is nothing short of extraordinary. By leveraging its advanced qubits, superconducting design, and error-correction capabilities, Willow has demonstrated the ability to perform random circuit sampling tasks in a fraction of the time that would be required by a classical supercomputer. Where the fastest classical supercomputer would take an unimaginably long 10^{25} years—about 100 million times longer than the age of the universe—Willow can complete the same task in under five minutes. This staggering difference in time is not just a technical achievement; it's a paradigm shift in how we think about computational power and its limitations.

The comparison of these two systems highlights the exponential growth in computational power that quantum computing promises. The gap in performance between classical and quantum systems in this context is so vast that it renders classical computers nearly irrelevant for solving certain classes of problems. This result underscores the power of quantum computing and the potential it has to transform industries and scientific fields that rely on computationally intensive tasks, such as drug discovery, climate modeling, financial forecasting, and artificial intelligence.

To fully appreciate the implications of this staggering performance difference, it's important to break down the calculation itself. In the case of the random circuit sampling task, Willow was able to complete the task in under five minutes, while the classical supercomputer's estimated time of 10^{25} years puts into perspective just how monumental the gap is. To visualize this, consider that 10^{25} years is an almost incomprehensible amount of time. The age of the universe itself is roughly 13.8 billion years, or 1.38×10^{10} years. So, the classical supercomputer would need 10^{25} years, which is 10,000,000,000,000,000,000,000,000 (10 sextillion) times longer than the entire age of the universe. This not only emphasizes the speed advantage of quantum computing but also highlights the inability of classical systems to even approach the scale of certain quantum calculations.

The implications of this performance gap are far-reaching. First and foremost, it shows that quantum computers like Willow are no longer just theoretical or experimental systems. They are already outpacing the fastest classical computers in terms of solving certain types of complex problems. This has profound consequences for industries that depend on rapid computational simulations and optimization processes. Industries like pharmaceuticals, where the design of new drugs requires immense computational resources, or energy, where the modeling of chemical reactions and energy flows could be accelerated exponentially, will see transformative effects. Similarly, quantum computing's ability to process vast amounts of data in real-time will revolutionize fields like artificial intelligence, making machine learning models more efficient and effective in tasks ranging from natural language processing to image recognition.

Moreover, the exponential growth in computational power that quantum computing enables isn't limited to a specific set of problems. It's a game-changer across a wide range of disciplines. In finance, for example, quantum algorithms could vastly improve the ability to model complex systems like stock markets, helping to predict price movements with far greater accuracy. In climate science, quantum simulations could provide insights into atmospheric conditions or climate models that were previously computationally prohibitive. The implications for fields like cryptography are similarly profound, where quantum computers could potentially break existing encryption systems, spurring the development of new, quantum-resistant encryption methods.

The shift from classical to quantum computing also offers a new level of scalability. Whereas classical computers are constrained by the limits of Moore's Law—the idea that computational power doubles roughly every two years—quantum computing promises an entirely new growth trajectory. By harnessing the inherent parallelism of quantum mechanics, quantum computers can perform operations on an exponentially larger scale than classical computers, opening up entirely new possibilities in computational power.

This exponential growth is perhaps the most exciting aspect of quantum computing's potential. Whereas classical computers are fundamentally constrained by physical limitations in hardware and processing power, quantum systems are only limited by the laws of quantum mechanics themselves—laws that, in theory, offer virtually unlimited potential for growth. The performance gap demonstrated by Willow in random circuit sampling is just a glimpse of what is to come. As quantum computing technology continues to evolve, we can expect this gap to widen, offering even more dramatic speedups for tasks that were once thought to be impossible or impractical.

In conclusion, the power of random circuit sampling and Willow's mind-blowing performance are clear indicators of the vast potential of quantum computing. This benchmark not only proves that quantum computers can already outperform classical systems for certain problems, but it also highlights the exponential growth in computational power that quantum systems offer. The implications of this shift will reverberate across industries, enabling faster, more accurate simulations and solving problems that were previously out of reach. Willow, as the latest manifestation of Google's quantum vision, is at the forefront of this revolution, demonstrating the extraordinary capabilities of quantum computing and setting the stage for even greater breakthroughs in the future.

Chapter 5: The Technology Behind Willow

The innovation behind Willow's performance lies in its unique design, specifically the use of tunable qubits and couplers. At the heart of these innovations is the ability to adjust the properties of the qubits and their connections, or couplings, allowing for extremely fast and low-error operations. In traditional quantum computing, qubits interact with each other in a fixed manner, meaning that if a qubit's interaction with its neighbor isn't perfectly tuned, the error rate increases. Willow's tunable qubits address this issue by enabling precise control over how qubits interact, or "couple," with each other, enhancing the accuracy of the computations. This adaptability is crucial for minimizing the errors that are inherent in quantum computing systems.

Tunable qubits work by allowing their energy levels and coupling strengths to be adjusted in real-time. This flexibility ensures that quantum gates—operations that manipulate qubits—can be performed with lower error rates. Since qubits are highly sensitive to their environment, even minor imperfections in their interaction can lead to significant errors. Willow's tunable couplers help to mitigate these errors by ensuring that qubits interact only when necessary and in the optimal way for the specific computation at hand. This contributes to a more reliable and stable quantum system, as qubits are constantly fine-tuned for maximum efficiency. As a result, Willow can perform complex operations with a higher degree of precision than earlier quantum chips, reducing the need for error correction and enhancing the overall performance of the system.

This tunability also has a profound impact on Willow's performance. By enabling fast, low-error operations, Willow can execute quantum algorithms more efficiently. The ability to optimize the interactions between qubits not only improves the overall computational speed but also reduces the likelihood of errors during processing. In practical terms, this means that Willow is more capable of performing large-scale computations and solving complex problems with greater accuracy, a significant improvement over previous quantum computers that suffered from higher error rates and slower operations.

Another key aspect of Willow's design is its reconfigurability. In traditional computers, hardware configurations are largely fixed once they are built, but quantum systems need to be flexible in order to adapt to the changing requirements of different quantum algorithms. Willow's reconfigurability allows its hardware to adapt in situ, meaning that it can adjust its configuration dynamically as needed for different tasks. This ability to reconfigure and optimize performance on the fly makes Willow highly versatile, as it can handle a broad range of applications without requiring a complete redesign of its physical hardware.

For example, when running a quantum algorithm, Willow's hardware can adjust itself to optimize the performance of certain operations or improve the accuracy of its qubits based on the algorithm's requirements. This kind of optimization is a significant advantage in quantum computing, where errors can accumulate quickly, and fine-tuning the hardware can make a noticeable difference in the results. By reconfiguring its hardware to match the needs of the algorithm in real-time, Willow can maximize its computational power, making it more efficient and reliable for a variety of use cases.

In addition to reconfigurability, qubit connectivity is another crucial factor in Willow's design. In quantum computing, connectivity refers to the number of interactions that each qubit can have with its neighboring qubits. The more qubits can interact with each other, the more efficiently complex algorithms can be expressed. Willow's design ensures that qubits are highly connected, allowing for greater flexibility in how quantum operations are structured and executed. This high connectivity is important for complex quantum algorithms, where qubits need to share information quickly and efficiently to produce accurate results.

Moreover, the importance of qubit connectivity becomes even more evident as the system scales. As more qubits are added to the quantum computer, the system's ability to maintain high connectivity without sacrificing performance is crucial for maintaining accuracy. If qubits are poorly connected, the algorithm's complexity increases, and errors become more likely. Willow's design ensures that as more qubits are added, their connectivity remains robust, meaning that the system can scale effectively without sacrificing the accuracy of the computation. This scalability is a fundamental characteristic that sets Willow apart from earlier quantum chips. It means that, as the demand for larger and more powerful quantum computers grows, Willow can scale up seamlessly without a significant increase in error rates or a loss of efficiency.

The scalability of Willow is a critical step toward making large-scale quantum computing a reality. As quantum computing moves from laboratory experiments to real-world applications, it is essential that quantum systems can grow in size and complexity while maintaining the same level of performance and reliability. Willow's ability to scale, with its high qubit connectivity and reconfigurable hardware, makes it a viable candidate for the next generation of quantum computers capable of solving real-world, computationally intensive problems.

In conclusion, Willow's innovative use of tunable qubits, reconfigurability, and qubit connectivity has propelled it to the forefront of quantum computing. These design choices have enabled it to perform faster, more accurate operations, and scale effectively as the number of qubits increases. By addressing some of the most significant challenges in quantum computing, such as error rates and scalability, Willow has set a new benchmark in the field and paved the way for more advanced and practical quantum computers in the future. Through these technological breakthroughs, Willow is not just a powerful quantum chip; it is a key step in realizing the full potential of quantum computing and unlocking new possibilities across industries and research fields.

.

Chapter 6: From Research to Practical Applications

As Willow continues to push the boundaries of quantum computing, its potential applications extend far beyond the realm of theoretical research. Industries across the globe are beginning to recognize the vast possibilities that quantum technology brings, and Willow, with its advanced capabilities, is positioned to revolutionize several key sectors.

One of the most promising areas for Willow's application lies in the pharmaceutical industry. Drug discovery is an inherently computationally demanding process, requiring the simulation of complex molecules and their interactions with biological systems. Traditional computers often struggle with the scale and complexity of these simulations, as the sheer number of potential molecular interactions makes it nearly impossible to test each one exhaustively. Willow, however, is capable of simulating molecular systems with unparalleled accuracy and speed. By enabling the rapid modeling of chemical reactions, it can drastically reduce the time and cost required to develop new drugs. Quantum computing could accelerate the process of finding viable drug candidates, potentially speeding up the development of treatments for diseases that have long eluded conventional approaches, such as cancer and neurological disorders.

Similarly, Willow's advanced computational capabilities have the potential to transform the energy sector. Battery technology, for example, is currently facing significant limitations. The development of new, more efficient batteries is a crucial challenge in the transition to renewable energy sources. Willow's ability to simulate complex materials at the quantum level could help identify new materials for batteries that are more energy-dense, longer-lasting, and environmentally friendly. Quantum computing can also aid in optimizing the design of power grids and renewable energy systems, improving the efficiency and reliability of these technologies as the world seeks to reduce its dependence on fossil fuels.

In the field of fusion power, where researchers are striving to replicate the energy production processes of the sun, Willow could help to solve some of the key challenges. Fusion reactions require incredibly high temperatures and pressures to occur, and simulating these conditions on a classical computer is exceedingly difficult. Willow, however, with its ability to model quantum systems and their interactions with extreme precision, could provide insights into how to stabilize plasma and optimize the conditions for sustained fusion reactions. This could bring humanity one step closer to achieving clean, virtually limitless energy.

Beyond its commercial applications, Willow's performance will have a profound impact on scientific research, enabling the exploration of complex problems that were once thought to be unsolvable. In climate science, for instance, quantum computing could revolutionize the way we model the Earth's atmosphere and predict changes in global weather patterns. The sheer complexity of these models—considering the many variables involved and their interactions—makes them difficult to simulate accurately with classical computers. By harnessing the power of quantum computing, Willow could provide scientists with the ability to simulate climate models with unprecedented precision, allowing for more accurate predictions about the effects of climate change and better-informed policy decisions.

Another area where Willow's capabilities will drive scientific discovery is in protein folding. This is one of the most complex challenges in biology, as the shape of a protein determines its function, and understanding this process is critical for fields like drug development and disease treatment. Classical computers struggle to simulate the folding process, given the immense number of possible configurations a protein can take. Quantum computers like Willow, however, have the potential to simulate these processes much more efficiently. This could lead to breakthroughs in our understanding of diseases caused by protein misfolding, such as Alzheimer's, and help to develop treatments for these conditions.

Space exploration is another field that will benefit from the power of Willow and quantum computing in general. The challenges of simulating interstellar environments, modeling the physics of black holes, and understanding the fundamental forces of the universe require computational capabilities far beyond what current systems can offer. Quantum computers like Willow could enable scientists to model the behavior of matter and energy in extreme conditions—whether within the cores of stars, in the presence of strong gravitational fields, or in the vacuum of space—allowing for more accurate simulations of space phenomena. This could lead to new insights into the fundamental workings of the universe and inform the next generation of space exploration missions.

Perhaps the most exciting aspect of quantum computing is its ability to solve problems that are otherwise deemed unsolvable by classical computers. These problems, often referred to as NP-hard or NP-complete problems, are characterized by their complexity and the sheer number of possible solutions that must be tested to find the optimal one. Classical computers can take an impractical amount of time to solve these problems, particularly as they scale up in size. Quantum computers, however, can exploit the principles of superposition and entanglement to explore multiple solutions simultaneously, dramatically reducing the time required to find the optimal answer.

Take the example of optimization problems, which are pervasive in fields ranging from logistics and supply chain management to finance and artificial intelligence. Finding the most efficient route for delivery trucks, optimizing financial portfolios, or designing the most effective machine learning algorithms all require solving complex optimization problems. For classical computers, these problems become increasingly difficult to solve as the number of variables increases. Quantum computers like Willow, however, are well-suited to tackle these problems efficiently, enabling businesses and researchers to find optimal solutions much more quickly than ever before.

In the realm of cryptography, quantum computing also has the potential to revolutionize security systems. Current encryption algorithms rely on the fact that classical computers cannot efficiently factor large numbers, a task that is central to public-key cryptography. Quantum computers, however, can perform these calculations exponentially faster than classical systems, which means that many of the current encryption methods could be easily broken by quantum computers. While this presents a challenge for existing security protocols, it also opens the door for new, quantum-resistant encryption methods that would be far more secure in the age of quantum computing.

Finally, case studies in the real world demonstrate the potential of quantum computers like Willow to solve previously intractable problems. For instance, researchers have already used quantum algorithms to simulate simple molecules and predict their behavior with greater accuracy than classical methods allow. As quantum computers improve, they will be able to simulate more complex systems, such as large proteins or entire chemical reactions, leading to breakthroughs in fields like material science, drug discovery, and environmental science.

In conclusion, the future of quantum computing, driven by Willow's advanced capabilities, holds the promise of solving some of the world's most pressing challenges. From revolutionizing industries like pharmaceuticals and energy to enabling breakthroughs in fundamental scientific research, quantum computing will transform our ability to solve problems that were once thought to be unsolvable. By addressing these "unsolvable" problems, Willow and other quantum computers will unlock new possibilities for the future, offering solutions that could have profound impacts on the way we live, work, and understand the universe itself.

Chapter 7: The Future of Quantum Computing

As Willow sets a new benchmark in the world of quantum computing, it represents not just a significant technological achievement but a stepping stone toward even greater advancements. Google's vision for the future of quantum computing goes far beyond the capabilities of Willow, laying out a roadmap that will lead to the development of larger, more powerful, and more fault-tolerant quantum systems.

Google's roadmap for quantum computing includes several ambitious milestones that will extend the capabilities of quantum chips beyond Willow. While Willow has made impressive strides in improving quantum coherence times, error correction, and computational speed, it is still just one phase in the journey toward truly scalable, fault-tolerant quantum computers.

One of the key areas of focus for Google and the broader quantum computing community is developing fault-tolerant quantum computers—systems that can operate reliably even as the number of qubits and their interactions grow. This will require breakthroughs in quantum error correction and the ability to maintain the integrity of qubits over long periods, a challenge that has long been a barrier to the practical use of quantum computers. Google's roadmap anticipates building quantum systems that can correct errors dynamically and automatically as they arise, ensuring that quantum computations remain accurate even in the face of noise and decoherence.

Google's focus on scaling up quantum systems is also a crucial next step. As the number of qubits in a quantum computer increases, the complexity of the system grows exponentially. Managing this complexity, both from a hardware and software perspective, will require significant innovation in how quantum chips are designed and fabricated. Willow represents a giant leap forward in this regard, but the future quantum chips will need to continue to scale, achieving not only more qubits but also enhanced connectivity, tunability, and reconfigurability to support larger and more complex algorithms.

Another area that Google is pursuing is the development of quantum processors that can handle real-world applications. As quantum computing moves from theoretical research to practical implementation, it will need to demonstrate its ability to solve real-world problems in areas like cryptography, material science, and artificial intelligence. The path to these applications involves building quantum computers that can operate on problems that are both larger in scale and more complex in their requirements, moving beyond the academic benchmarks to create systems capable of delivering tangible benefits to industries and society.

Despite the tremendous potential of quantum computing, the road to making quantum computers commercially viable is filled with challenges. The first and most obvious hurdle is the cost and complexity of building and maintaining quantum hardware. Unlike classical computers, which rely on silicon-based circuits, quantum computers require highly specialized components and materials that can withstand the extreme conditions necessary for quantum phenomena to occur, such as ultra-cold temperatures and vacuum environments. The fabrication of quantum chips is a complex and expensive process, and scaling up production to meet the demands of commercial applications presents significant technical and economic challenges.

Moreover, there is the challenge of creating a quantum software ecosystem that can support a wide range of applications. While classical computers have a robust software environment that supports everything from operating systems to specialized applications, quantum computing is still in the early stages of software development. Programming quantum computers requires a new way of thinking, as quantum algorithms differ fundamentally from classical algorithms. Developing a quantum programming language, as well as software tools and libraries that can help developers build practical quantum applications, is a key area of focus. However, the current state of quantum software is still in its infancy, and bridging the gap between quantum hardware and software is essential for enabling the commercial use of quantum computers.

A significant part of the journey toward quantum commercialization will also involve addressing the workforce gap in quantum computing. As quantum computing continues to evolve, there will be an increasing demand for skilled professionals who can design, develop, and operate quantum systems. This includes not only quantum physicists and engineers but also software developers, mathematicians, and data scientists who are equipped to work with quantum algorithms and integrate them into real-world applications. This workforce development will be crucial in ensuring that quantum computing can transition from research labs to industries that will benefit from it.

Finally, the role of governments and researchers in this journey cannot be overstated. While private companies like Google are making significant investments in quantum technology, the commercial viability of quantum computing will also require collaboration between the public and private sectors. Governments around the world are increasingly recognizing the strategic importance of quantum computing and are investing in quantum research and development through grants, partnerships, and initiatives. Additionally, international cooperation among researchers and companies will be vital in overcoming the many technical challenges associated with quantum computing.

Looking forward, the next 10, 20, and 50 years in quantum computing promise to be a period of extraordinary innovation and transformation. Quantum computing is poised to disrupt a wide range of industries, from healthcare to finance, and from logistics to artificial intelligence, creating entirely new paradigms of problem-solving and driving forward a new era of technological advancement.

In the next 10 years, quantum computing will likely transition from a research tool to a practical technology used in select industries. We can expect to see the first quantum computers solve real-world problems that are too complex for classical systems. In fields like drug discovery, material science, and climate modeling, quantum algorithms will begin to make meaningful contributions by providing more accurate simulations and optimizing processes in ways that were previously unthinkable. Quantum computing will also have a profound impact on cybersecurity, where it will be used to develop new encryption methods that can protect data in an age of quantum threats.

Over the next 20 years, as quantum computing becomes more scalable and accessible, it will transform industries at a much larger scale. In finance, for instance, quantum computers will revolutionize risk modeling, asset management, and fraud detection, enabling financial institutions to make more informed decisions in real-time. In manufacturing, quantum computing will allow for more efficient supply chains, optimized production schedules, and improved quality control. Additionally, quantum computing will fuel advances in artificial intelligence, enabling the development of more powerful machine learning algorithms that can process data faster and with greater accuracy than ever before.

Looking 50 years into the future, quantum computing could fundamentally reshape our society and economy. As quantum systems become more integrated into our daily lives, we could see breakthroughs in energy production, with quantum simulations leading to new, more efficient forms of energy generation and storage. In healthcare, quantum computers could be used to develop personalized treatments and cures for diseases, drastically improving quality of life. Even in fields like space exploration, quantum computing could enable the development of advanced propulsion systems, new materials for spacecraft, and more accurate models of the universe, propelling humanity into a new age of exploration.

In conclusion, while the road ahead is filled with challenges, the next few decades will see quantum computing unlock a new wave of innovation that will transform industries and scientific fields. Google's Willow chip is a pivotal step in this journey, but it is just one part of a much larger story that will unfold over the coming years. As the technology matures and becomes more accessible, the possibilities for what quantum computers can achieve are virtually limitless, making this an exciting time for both researchers and industries alike. The quantum age is on the horizon, and its impact will be felt across the globe, creating a future where problems once thought unsolvable are within reach of being solved.

Conclusion

As we stand on the threshold of a new era in computing, the release of Google's Willow chip marks not only a milestone in the field of quantum computing but also the beginning of a transformative revolution that will reshape industries, accelerate scientific discovery, and unlock solutions to some of the world's most pressing challenges. Willow is more than just a powerful quantum chip—it is the embodiment of years of research, innovation, and breakthroughs that push the boundaries of what was once thought possible in computational science. The implications of Willow's advancements are profound, and its contribution to the quantum revolution will be felt across a multitude of sectors for decades to come.

Willow represents a significant leap forward in quantum computing technology. With its enhanced coherence times, reduced error rates, and the ability to perform complex computations far beyond the capabilities of classical supercomputers, Willow signals the dawn of a new era in computing. It offers the promise of solving problems that were previously unsolvable by classical systems, from simulating molecular interactions in drug development to optimizing energy systems and tackling the complexities of climate modeling. Willow's breakthroughs lay the groundwork for quantum computers that can address real-world challenges and drive advancements in fields as diverse as healthcare, energy, materials science, and artificial intelligence.

But the impact of Willow is not limited to these immediate applications. By pushing the boundaries of quantum coherence and error correction, Willow has set a new standard for what is possible in quantum computation, opening the door to future systems that can solve even more complex problems. As quantum computers continue to evolve, they will increasingly become integral tools in a wide range of industries, driving innovations that were once considered out of reach.

However, while Willow is a monumental achievement, it is only the beginning. The true potential of quantum computing lies in continued research and development. As the technology matures, new breakthroughs in quantum error correction, qubit scaling, and hardware optimization will make quantum computers even more powerful, reliable, and commercially viable. The continued evolution of quantum computing systems like Willow will ultimately lead to the creation of large-scale, fault-tolerant quantum computers that can solve the most complex problems humanity faces.

Google's long-term commitment to quantum computing is evident in its continued investment in research, development, and infrastructure. As demonstrated by the creation of Willow and the advancements it brings, Google is at the forefront of this quantum revolution, and its vision for the future is one of leadership, innovation, and collaboration. Google understands that quantum computing is not just a technological breakthrough—it is an opportunity to reshape the world and address challenges that were once beyond our reach.

Looking ahead, Google's vision for the future of quantum computing extends beyond the immediate capabilities of Willow. The company is focused on creating scalable, fault-tolerant quantum computers that can be applied to real-world problems across industries. Google's investment in quantum hardware and software, as well as its partnerships with academic institutions and governments, reflects its recognition of the importance of quantum computing for the future of technology and science.

By pushing the boundaries of quantum systems and developing new techniques for error correction, qubit control, and algorithmic optimization, Google is shaping the quantum computing landscape for years to come. Its vision is to not only build the hardware necessary for quantum computation but also to develop the ecosystem of software, tools, and methodologies that will allow quantum computers to be applied in practical, impactful ways. Google's goal is to create a world where quantum computers are as accessible and indispensable as classical systems are today, with applications that solve some of the most pressing problems facing humanity.

The transformative potential of quantum computing goes beyond the immediate impact of Willow or any single quantum chip. Quantum technology, in its entirety, has the potential to radically change the way we understand the world around us and how we solve the challenges that lie ahead. From advancing our ability to model the most complex systems in science to enabling breakthroughs in healthcare, energy, and artificial intelligence, quantum computing will drive innovations that have the power to change the fabric of our society.

In healthcare, for example, quantum computers like Willow could accelerate drug discovery and personalize treatments for patients, opening the door to cures for diseases that have long eluded researchers. In energy, quantum computing could enable more efficient, sustainable solutions for powering the planet, helping to address the challenges of climate change and energy scarcity. The possibilities are virtually endless, and as quantum computers continue to improve, they will increasingly be relied upon to solve some of the world's most difficult problems.

Quantum computing also offers the potential for a paradigm shift in how we approach scientific discovery. By enabling researchers to simulate complex systems with unprecedented accuracy, quantum computers will provide new insights into the workings of the universe. From unraveling the mysteries of dark matter and black holes to simulating the behavior of molecules and materials, quantum technology will revolutionize our understanding of the natural world and unlock new frontiers in science.

Moreover, the journey of quantum computing is not one that can be undertaken by any single company or nation. It will require global collaboration, with researchers, scientists, and policymakers working together to build the infrastructure, standards, and ethical frameworks necessary to guide the development and deployment of quantum technologies. This collaborative effort will ensure that the benefits of quantum computing are shared by all and that the technology is used for the greater good of humanity.

In conclusion, Willow is a major step forward in the journey of quantum computing, but it is just the beginning. The future of quantum technology is one of immense potential, where innovations in computing will drive progress in every aspect of our lives, from science and medicine to energy and security. Google's commitment to pushing the boundaries of quantum computing is shaping the future of this transformative technology, and as we look ahead, it is clear that quantum computing will play an increasingly central role in solving the world's most pressing challenges. We are entering an era where the impossible becomes possible, and the impact of quantum technology will be felt across generations. The quantum revolution is here, and it is only just beginning.

08